AF480649

# THE WARRIOR'S MANTRA

## DECIPHERING THE HANUMAN CHALISA

DR. MINAKSHI BANSAL

ᘐᘐᘐ

# Contents

# Contents

# Prayer

*||Doha||*

*Shri Guru Charan Saroj Raj*
*Nij mane mukure sudhar*
*Barnao Raghuvar Bimal Jasu*
*Jo dayaku phal chari*

*Budhi Hin Tanu Janike*
*Sumirau Pavan Kumar*
*Bal budhi Vidya dehu mohi*
*Harahu Kalesa Vikar*

*||Chaupai||*

*Jai Hanuman gyan gun sagar*
*Jai Kapis tihun lok ujagar*

*Ram doot atulit bal dhama*
*Anjani-putra Pavan sut nama*

*Mahavir Bikram Bajrangi*
*Kumati nivar sumati Ke sangi*

*Kanchan varan viraj subesa*
*Kanan Kundal Kunchit Kesa*

*Hath Vajra Aur Dhuvaje Viraje*
*Kandhe moonj janehu sajai*

*Sankar suvan kesri Nandan*
*Tej pratap muha Jag vandan*

*Vidyavan guni ati chatur*
*Ram kaj karibe ko aatur*

*Prabu charitra sunibe ko rasiya*
*Ram Lakhan Sita man Basiya*

*Sukshma roop dhari Siyahi dikhava*
*Vikat roop dhari lanka jarava*

*Bhima roop dhari asur sanghare*
*Ramachandra ke kaj sanvare*

*Laye Sanjivan Lakhan Jiyaye*
*Shri Raghuvir Harashi ur laye*

*Raghupati Kinhi bahut badai*
*Tum mam priye Bharat-hi sam bhai*

*Sahas badan tumharo yash gaave*
*As kahi Shripati kanth lagaave*

*Sankadik Brahmadi Muneesa*
*Narad Sarad sahit Aheesa*

*Yam Kuber Digpal Jahan te*
*Kavi kovid kahi sake kahan te*

*Tum upkar Sugreevahin keenha*
*Ram milaye rajpad deenha*

*Tumharo mantra Vibheeshan mana*
*Lankeshwar Bhaye Sub jag jana*

PRAYER

*Yug sahastra jojan par Bhanu*
*Leelyo tahi madhur phal janu*

*Prabhu mudrika meli mukh mahee*
*Jaladhi langhi gaye achraj nahee*

*Durgaam kaj jagat ke jete*
*Sugam anugraha tumhre tete*

*Ram dware tum rakhvare,*
*Hoat na agya binu paisare*

*Sub sukh lahai tumhari sarna*
*Tum rakshak kahu ko dar na*

*Aapan tej samharo aapai*
*Teenhon lok hank te kanpai*

*Bhoot pisach Nikat nahin aavai*
*Mahavir jab naam sunavai*

*Nase rog harai sab peera*
*Japat nirantar Hanumant beera*

*Sankat se Hanuman chudavai*
*Man Karam Vachan dyan jo lavai*

*Sub par Ram tapasvee raja*
*Tin ke kaj sakal Tum saja*

*Aur manorath jo koi lavai*
*Sohi amit jeevan phal pavai*

*Charon Yug partap tumhara*

*Hai persidh jagat ujiyara*

*Sadhu Sant ke tum Rakhware*
*Asur nikandan Ram dulhare*

*Ashta sidhi nav nidhi ke dhata*
*As var deen Janki mata*

*Ram rasayan tumhare pasa*
*Sada raho Raghupati ke dasa*

*Tumhare bhajan Ram ko pavai*
*Janam janam ke dukh bisravai*

*Anth kaal Raghuvir pur jayee*
*Jahan janam Hari-Bakht Kahayee*

*Aur Devta Chit na dharehi*
*Hanumanth se hi sarve sukh karehi*

*Sankat kate mite sab peera*
*Jo sumirai Hanumat Balbeera*

*Jai Jai Jai Hanuman Gosahin*
*Kripa Karahu Gurudev ki nyahin*

*Jo sat bar path kare kohi*
*Chutehi bandhi maha sukh hohi*

*Jo yah padhe Hanuman Chalisa*
*Hoye siddhi sakhi Gaureesa*

*Tulsidas sada hari chera*
*Keejai Das Hrdaye mein dera*

• x •

**॥Doha॥**

*Pavantnai sankar haran,*
*Mangal murti roop.*
*Ram Lakhan Sita sahit,*
*Hrdaye basahu sur bhoop.*

❦❦❦

# About The Author

Dr. Minakshi Bansal, born in the bustling metropolis of Delhi, India, has led a life steeped in artistry, scholarly pursuit, and an unwavering commitment to societal betterment. Following her marriage, she relocated to Ahmedabad, Gujarat, where she has since blossomed into a multifaceted beacon of inspiration for many. Dr. Minakshi is not only recognized as a gifted artist in the realm of Fine Arts but also as an esteemed author, a devoted social worker and a dedicated research scholar in Psychology. Her journey, marked by a profound dedication to elevating those around her, especially the downtrodden and underprivileged children of society, is a testament to her deep-seated belief in the transformative power of engagement and empathy.

From her earliest days, Minakshi was distinguished by an insatiable appetite for reading. Her literary universe was inhabited by characters and narratives that spanned ethical tales, motivational and inspirational stories, and the mythic parables imbued with life lessons. This voracious reading habit was not merely for personal edification but was driven by a desire to distill and disseminate the essence of these narratives to foster the development of students and peers alike. She was particularly captivated by the lives and teachings of historical figures and spiritual leaders such as Adi Shankaracharya, Swami Vivekananda, Dr. APJ Abdul Kalam, Mahamana Pandit Madan Mohan Malviya, Mahatma Gandhi, Sardar Vallabhai Patel, and Vinoba Bhave, among others. Their philosophies and life stories fueled her ambition to embody their ideals of resilience, selflessness, and relentless pursuit of knowledge.

Dr. Minakshi's academic and practical engagement with psychology has been equally noteworthy. As a research scholar, her focus has been on exploring the intricate tapestry of the human psyche, aiming to unlock the potential for psychological well-being and societal harmony. Her scholarly work is complemented by her active involvement in social work, where she employs her academic insights to make tangible differences in the lives of the underprivileged. Her endeavours in social work are characterized by an innovative approach that combines traditional wisdom with contemporary psychological practices to address the multifaceted challenges faced by these communities.

Her artistic talents, another facet of her diverse capabilities, are not merely a personal passion but also serve as a medium through which she communicates and connects with others. Her art, rich in symbolism and emotional depth, reflects her philosophical inquiries and social concerns, offering viewers a glimpse into the breadth of her intellect and the depth of her compassion.

In addition to her contributions to the arts and social sciences, Dr. Minakshi has embraced the healing arts of Pranic Healing, mastering the techniques developed by Master Choa Kok Sui. This practice, which focuses on the manipulation of Prana or life energy to heal the body and aura, has been both a personal journey of discovery and a means through which she extends her healing touch to others. Her proficiency in Pranic Healing is complemented by her advocacy and teaching of various forms of meditation aimed at rejuvenation, personal betterment, and the cultivation of harmony within individuals and communities alike.

Dr. Minakshi's life is a narrative of relentless pursuit, not just of personal achievement but of the upliftment and empowerment of society at large. Her diverse interests and talents—spanning the arts, literature, psychology, and the healing practices—converge on a singular path of service. She embodies the spirit of the luminaries who inspired her, channelling their legacy through her actions and teachings. Through her books, art, and social initiatives, she continues to inspire a new generation to embark on their own journeys of self-discovery, resilience, and altruism.

Her commitment to social betterment, particularly her focus on uplifting underprivileged children, reflects a deep understanding of the transformative potential of education and personal development. By integrating her knowledge of psychology, her artistic sensibilities, and her healing practices, Dr. Bansal has developed a holistic approach to social work that addresses both the immediate needs and the long-term well-being of the communities she serves.

As an author, Dr. Minakshi's writings offer a blend of inspirational insights, practical wisdom, and reflective contemplations drawn from her extensive reading and life experiences. Her books serve as a guide for those seeking to navigate the complexities of life with grace, resilience, and purpose. Through her narratives, she extends an invitation to her readers to explore the depths of their own potential and to contribute meaningfully to the collective well-being of society.

In Dr. Minakshi Bansal, we find a remarkable synthesis of the artist, the scholar, the healer, and the social activist. Her life's work stands as a beacon of hope and a source of inspiration for individuals seeking to make a difference in the world. Her story is a compelling reminder of the power of individual action, rooted in compassion and driven by a profound commitment to the betterment of humanity. Dr. Minakshi's legacy is not just in the tangible outcomes of her efforts but in the enduring spirit of inquiry, empathy, and service that she embodies.

ৡৡৡ

# Preface

From the dimly lit corners of childhood memories where the echoing chants of the "Hanuman Chalisa" first resonated, to the bustling realities of modern life, the hymn has followed me like a shadow, sometimes a whisper, at other times a guide. This book has grown out of a deep reverence for this ancient text and an enduring curiosity about the enduring wisdom embedded in its verses. As a little girl, I watched elders recite the hymn with an air of solemnity and devotion, their voices filled with an inexplicable power that seemed to both calm the air and invigorate the soul. This mystery—the profound emotional and spiritual resonance of the "Hanuman Chalisa"—became the seed for a much larger exploration into the life and lessons of Hanuman, a deity revered across centuries for his strength, valor, and fidelity.

In "The Warrior's Mantra," I delve into each verse of the "Hanuman Chalisa," seeking to uncover how ancient words translate into timeless wisdom. This is not just a book of spiritual or religious commentary; it is an invitation to explore how the qualities of a mythological figure can inform our modern lives, providing insights into resilience, courage, loyalty, and humility. Hanuman's story, from his miraculous birth to his indomitable adventures in the epic Ramayana, offers more than just tales of divine feats; they provide a blueprint for personal growth and spiritual fortitude.

This exploration is rooted in a personal journey, woven through with the threads of academic inquiry and reflective meditation. By dissecting the "Hanuman Chalisa" verse by verse, I aim to present a comprehensive view that intertwines the historical and mythological origins of the hymn with practical applications for contemporary life. Each verse is a lesson in virtue and strategy, revealing that true strength is as much about moral integrity and selflessness as it is about physical prowess and daring.

The narrative of Hanuman teaches us that being a warrior is not merely about battling external foes but also about confronting the internal adversaries of fear, ignorance, and selfishness. Hanuman embodies the ideal balance of brawn and wisdom, power and grace, serving as a perfect archetype for anyone striving to overcome personal challenges and societal constraints. His devotion to Lord Rama is not just a tale of spiritual fervor but a testament to the transformative power of loyalty and love.

Through the pages of this book, I explore how devotion can be a powerful catalyst for change—not just spiritually but in very tangible, practical ways. Devotion, as demonstrated by Hanuman, involves a profound commitment to the welfare of others, viewing service as a pathway to enlightenment. This book makes the case that such timeless virtues are not only relevant but essential in a world that often prizes individualism over community and material success over moral development.

Furthermore, the act of revisiting and interpreting the "Hanuman Chalisa" serves as a personal and collective meditation, a spiritual exercise that reinforces the values of diligence and mindfulness. The process of writing this book has been an exercise in devotion itself—an attempt to translate respect and reverence into understanding and insight.

As we journey through the verses together, this book invites readers to reflect on their own lives, to find their own version of strength and devotion, and perhaps to discover a little bit of Hanuman within themselves. Whether one is drawn to this book out of spiritual curiosity, scholarly interest, or a search for personal guidance, the goal is the same: to inspire a deeper engagement with life's trials and triumphs through the lens of ancient wisdom.

In crafting this narrative, my hope is that you, the reader, will find

"The Warrior's Mantra" not just instructive but transformative, offering a new perspective on how to navigate the complexities of modern existence with grace and fortitude. Let us embark on this journey not just as passive observers but as active participants, eager to uncover the riches of the "Hanuman Chalisa" and to apply its lessons in ways that resonate with and enrich our lives.

*Dr. Minakshi Bansal*
*Social Activist*
*Ahmedabad, Gujarat, Bharat*

❧❧❧

# 1: Invocation to Hanuman

*The opening verses of the "Hanuman Chalisa" serve as a powerful invocation, setting a spiritual foundation for the hymn. This invocation is not only a call for Hanuman's blessings but also an expression of the deep respect and veneration he commands. The act of invoking Hanuman at the beginning of any endeavor is seen as auspicious, providing the devotee with spiritual strength and support. This practice emphasizes the significance of beginning spiritual practices with an invocation to ensure success and divine backing.*

***Verses 1-2:*** *Introduction and praise of Hanuman's powers.*

*Explores the significance of invoking Hanuman's name for spiritual strength and the power of starting spiritual practices with an invocation.*

ᐠᐠᐠ

# ONE

# INVOCATION TO HANUMAN

The "Hanuman Chalisa" begins with a profound invocation that sets the tone for the entire hymn. This initial dedication is more than just an introduction; it is a spiritual summons that resonates deeply with those seeking strength and courage in their lives. The first two verses of the Chalisa highlight the immense powers of Hanuman, an embodiment of devotion, strength, and loyalty. This invocation serves as a reminder of the potent energies Hanuman represents, urging devotees to call upon his name for guidance and protection.

Invoking Hanuman's name at the beginning of spiritual practices is a traditional way to harness his blessings. This act is not merely a formality but a deep, intentional connection that cultivates a sacred space for worship and reflection. It underscores the importance of starting any endeavor with a clear mind and a focused heart, seeking the divine support that Hanuman provides. The invocation acts as a spiritual anchor, offering stability and confidence to the devotee through the symbolic presence of Hanuman.

As the Chalisa unfolds, the invocation of Hanuman is not just about seeking his help but also about emulating his qualities. Hanuman's attributes of immense strength, fearless courage, and profound devotion to Lord Rama are qualities that every human can aspire to develop. This hymn, therefore, does more than just praise a deity; it guides the devotee on a path of personal evolution and spiritual growth.

## Understanding the Verses

Each verse of the Hanuman Chalisa is layered with symbolism and deeper meaning. The praises sung for Hanuman are not only about his physical might but also about his spiritual stature and his role as a remover of obstacles. He is described as someone who can alter forms at will, move mountains, dart through the air, and wield his powers with wisdom and humility. These descriptions are metaphorical teachings that encourage followers to internalize and manifest the virtues of wisdom, humility, strength, and devotion in their own lives.

Moreover, these verses highlight Hanuman's unique role in the epic Ramayana, where he was instrumental in the search for Sita and the defeat of Ravana. This narrative context serves as a backdrop for the devotee, offering rich insights into how challenges can be met with integrity and faith. As each verse unfolds, it reveals layers of spiritual wisdom, emphasizing the transformative power of devotion and the importance of selfless service.

## Applying the Teachings

The teachings of the Hanuman Chalisa are timeless and carry profound implications for contemporary life. In today's fast-paced world, where stress and anxiety are commonplace, the Chalisa serves as a source of comfort and strength. It teaches us that courage and humility can coexist, that true strength is about moral integrity, and that serving others selflessly can lead to immense personal and spiritual fulfillment.

Through the daily recitation or meditation on these verses, individuals can cultivate a more mindful and compassionate approach to life. The qualities of Hanuman – his strength, courage, devotion, and humility – become more than just spiritual concepts; they turn into practical attributes that can guide one's actions and interactions in the world.

By embracing these teachings, devotees learn to navigate life's challenges with grace and fortitude, inspired by Hanuman's example. The lessons woven through the Hanuman Chalisa encourage a life of service, reminding us that our actions can have a significant impact on the world around us. They also teach us that in the face of adversity, we can draw upon our inner strength and the divine support that invocation brings.

In essence, the Hanuman Chalisa is a spiritual guidebook that offers more than just praise for a revered deity; it provides a blueprint for living a life enriched with spiritual and moral values. The initial invocation sets the stage for a deeper engagement with these teachings, inviting the devotee to embark on a transformative journey. Through the verses of this sacred hymn, the pathway to courage, devotion, and peace is illuminated, offering solace and inspiration to all who traverse it. Thus, by integrating the essence of these teachings into daily life, one can achieve a balance of strength and serenity, empowered by the enduring spirit of Hanuman.

 PPP

## 2: Hanuman's Devotion

*Verses 3 and 4 celebrate Hanuman's unwavering devotion to Lord Rama, highlighting his role as an exemplary devotee. His dedication is portrayed as the ideal blend of strength and humility, serving as a guiding light for all who seek to deepen their own paths of devotion. This devotion is not passive but active, marked by deeds that demonstrate his commitment and loyalty, teaching us the power of devoted service.*

**Verses 3-4:** *Hanuman's devotion to Rama and his role as a devotee.*

*Discusses the virtues of devotion and loyalty, using Hanuman's example to inspire similar feelings in the reader's personal and spiritual life.*

ɷɷɷ

# TWO

# HANUMAN'S DEVOTION

Hanuman's devotion to Lord Rama represents a central theme within the "Hanuman Chalisa" and is a cornerstone in the exploration of the virtues of devotion and loyalty. Verses 3 and 4 of the hymn delve deeply into Hanuman's unwavering commitment to Rama, portraying him not only as a powerful entity but also as a paragon of devotion. His role as a devotee underscores a profound spiritual narrative that has inspired millions over centuries.

In these verses, Hanuman's actions, choices, and sacrifices in the epic Ramayana are recounted, demonstrating his loyalty and the lengths he was willing to go to serve Lord Rama. This aspect of the "Hanuman Chalisa" elevates the concept of devotion from a mere emotional or spiritual expression to a tangible and impactful force in the world. It positions Hanuman as a model for how deep devotion can positively influence one's conduct and the lives of others.

**The Essence of Devotion**

The essence of Hanuman's devotion lies in his selflessness and his readiness to serve without any desire for personal gain. His love for

Rama is not conditional or self-serving; it is pure and unconditional, driven by a deep spiritual connection rather than material or ephemeral rewards. This kind of devotion is powerful, transformative, and exceedingly rare. It offers a stark contrast to many of today's relationships, whether personal, professional, or spiritual, which are often governed by what one can gain rather than what one can give.

Hanuman's dedication is also marked by humility and reverence, qualities that amplify the strength of his devotion. Despite his immense power, he chooses service over sovereignty, assisting Rama not as a servant but as a devotee. This distinction is crucial because it elevates his actions from duty to devotion, infusing them with profound respect and love.

**Learning from Hanuman's Example**

By studying Hanuman's devotion, individuals are invited to reflect on their relationships and consider how devotion and loyalty play roles in their own lives. Hanuman's example prompts questions about the nature and quality of our loyalties—are they conditional, self-serving, or do they elevate the well-being of others? His life serves as a reminder that true devotion enriches and fulfills not only the recipient but also the giver.

In personal relationships, Hanuman's example can inspire a more selfless approach, where the happiness and well-being of loved ones become a priority. In professional contexts, it encourages a dedication to one's duties that goes beyond contractual obligations, driven by a commitment to excellence and integrity.

**Devotion in Spiritual Life**

In the spiritual dimension, Hanuman's devotion offers profound lessons about the path to divine connection and enlightenment. His relationship with Rama illuminates the spiritual efficacy of bhakti (devotion) as a means to attain spiritual insight and emotional fulfilment. The devotion Hanuman displays can be interpreted as bhakti yoga, one of the paths in Hinduism that emphasizes loving engagement with a personal god.

This spiritual approach is not just about worship in temples or at shrines; it is about living one's entire life in a spirit of service and devotion to a higher power, seeing and serving this divine presence in all aspects of life. This can profoundly alter how one interacts with the world, fostering a more compassionate, patient, and understanding attitude.

**Impact on Contemporary Life**

In a contemporary setting, Hanuman's devotion offers a template for resilience and strength in facing life's challenges. His courage and resourcefulness in overcoming obstacles during his service to Rama provide practical and spiritual strategies for dealing with personal hardships. Furthermore, his unwavering faith in the face of daunting challenges serves as a source of inspiration for maintaining hope and determination.

Adopting a mindset of devotion can lead to a life that not only seeks personal success but also contributes to the welfare of the community. This shift in perspective can lead to a more harmonious and compassionate society, as individuals inspired by Hanuman's example strive to act with integrity and benevolence.

In essence, the verses of the "Hanuman Chalisa" that focus on Hanuman's devotion do more than narrate historical spiritual feats; they serve as a guide for infusing one's life with the profound virtues of devotion and loyalty. By embodying these qualities, individuals can experience a richer, more meaningful existence, marked by deeper relationships and a resilient, compassionate spirit. Through Hanuman's example, we see that devotion is not a weakness but a formidable strength that can inspire change and foster a more fulfilling life.

৶৶৶

### 3: Hanuman's Might and Wisdom

*In verses 5 and 6, Hanuman's remarkable combination of physical strength and intellectual prowess is detailed. His ability to tactically overcome challenges and his insightful nature make him a unique figure in Hindu mythology, capable of both brute force and profound wisdom. This dual capability serves as an important lesson in balancing strength with intellect in our daily challenges.*

**Verses 5-6:** *Hanuman's strength, wisdom, and celibacy.*

*Connects his physical and mental prowess to the discipline and wisdom in handling life's challenges.*

ᗡᗡᗡ

# THREE

# HANUMAN'S MIGHT AND WISDOM

Verses 5 and 6 of the "Hanuman Chalisa" delve into the impressive attributes of Hanuman's physical strength, intellectual wisdom, and his choice of celibacy. These aspects not only define Hanuman as a unique deity in the Hindu pantheon but also serve as a guide for personal discipline and the wise management of life's challenges. Hanuman's extraordinary capabilities are not merely to be admired but are reflections of deeper spiritual truths and practical wisdom that can be applied in everyday life.

**The Integration of Strength and Wisdom**

Hanuman's physical might is legendary, as exemplified in his feats in the Ramayana, where he leapt oceans and moved mountains. However, his strength is always guided by a profound wisdom and a keen intellect. This combination of might and wisdom illustrates that true strength is more than physical capabilities—it also involves the intellectual and moral strength to use such power wisely and judiciously.

Hanuman's use of his strength, always in the service of good and under the guidance of his intellect and devotion, underscores the virtue of restraint and the responsible use of one's abilities.

In the context of personal development, Hanuman's example teaches that developing one's abilities and strengths should go hand in hand with cultivating wisdom. It's not enough to be strong or capable; one must also have the wisdom to use these strengths appropriately.

This teaches a balance that is crucial in all areas of life, from personal relationships to professional environments. For instance, in leadership, the balance of strength and wisdom mirrors Hanuman's role as a supporter of Rama, using his abilities not for personal gain but for supporting his lord and his companions.

## Celibacy as Discipline

Hanuman's celibacy is particularly significant, representing his complete devotion and the sublimation of his physical powers into spiritual energy. In Hindu philosophy, celibacy is often seen as a form of self-discipline that conserves physical energy and redirects it towards spiritual growth. Hanuman's choice of celibacy is aligned with his role as a devotee and his supernatural accomplishments, which are believed to be made possible by his immense control over his desires and his focused spiritual practice.

This aspect of Hanuman's life has profound implications for understanding how discipline and mastery over one's impulses can lead to greater achievements. In a world where instant gratification is often the norm, the principle of celibacy can be extended to mean a general mastery over one's desires and impulses, highlighting the importance of self-control and delayed gratification.

This can be particularly empowering when facing modern challenges related to excess and overindulgence, whether in terms of consumption, entertainment, or even the use of technology.

## Wisdom in Everyday Life

The wisdom of Hanuman also extends to his understanding and insight into complex situations. He always knew the best course of action during the adventures in the Ramayana, which often required not just strength but also clever thinking and diplomacy.

This intellectual prowess can be a source of inspiration for individuals facing difficult decisions or complex problems. It suggests that wisdom is not just about knowledge but also about applying this knowledge effectively to solve problems and navigate challenges.

Hanuman's intelligence was not just for problem-solving; it also involved a deep understanding of people, which enabled him to act with compassion and empathy. This is another layer of wisdom that is essential in today's world, where understanding and relating to others is crucial in both personal and professional realms.

## Applying Hanuman's Principles Today

Integrating Hanuman's strength, wisdom, and discipline into one's life can lead to a more balanced and fulfilled existence. By developing physical and intellectual capacities while also maintaining self-control and discipline, one can achieve not only personal and professional success but also a harmonious and ethical life.

Hanuman's life encourages a holistic approach to personal development—one that includes physical health, intellectual growth, and moral integrity.

Incorporating these lessons from Hanuman can transform how one handles life's pressures and challenges. By aspiring to his levels of physical strength and mental acumen, while also embracing his profound sense of duty and service, individuals can navigate their journeys more successfully and meaningfully. Hanuman's legacy, as captured in these verses of the "Hanuman Chalisa," continues to inspire a balanced approach to life that harmonizes strength with wisdom, power with compassion, and personal success with spiritual growth.

ᐅᐅᐅ

## 4: The Messenger of Strength

*Verses 7 and 8 focus on Hanuman as the messenger of Lord Rama, showcasing his role in carrying messages and representing Rama across various realms. His effectiveness as a messenger is attributed to his eloquence, courage, and discretion. This portrayal underscores the importance of communication and responsibility in leadership roles, suggesting that true messengers are those who can convey messages with integrity and tact.*

**Verses 7-8:** *Hanuman as the messenger of Lord Rama.*

*Highlights the importance of communication and responsibility in leadership roles.*

ᐅᐅᐅ

# FOUR

# THE MESSENGER OF STRENGTH

Verses 7 and 8 of the "Hanuman Chalisa" introduce Hanuman in a pivotal role as the messenger of Lord Rama, marking a significant theme that resonates deeply with the principles of communication and responsibility in leadership. This role is not just a title or function; it symbolizes Hanuman's ability to bridge distances, connect hearts, and transmit vital messages under challenging circumstances. It highlights his strength not only in physical terms but also in his capacity to serve and lead through effective communication.

**Hanuman's Role as a Messenger**

In the epic Ramayana, Hanuman's role as a messenger comes to the forefront during his mission to Lanka. Here, he is tasked with locating Sita and delivering Rama's message to her. This episode is not merely a demonstration of his loyalty and bravery but also showcases his tact, intelligence, and ability to communicate effectively. Hanuman proves his mettle as a messenger when he overcomes numerous obstacles to finally meet Sita in Ashoka Vatika, where he delivers Rama's message with empathy and assurance.

This role of Hanuman underscores the critical importance of communication in any leadership role. Effective communication involves clarity, empathy, and the ability to listen and respond appropriately. Hanuman's communication with Sita is particularly notable for its compassion and reassurance, qualities that are indispensable for any leader.

## Communication as a Leadership Skill

Effective leadership is heavily reliant on good communication skills. Leaders, like messengers, must convey information clearly and persuasively, but they must also be adept at listening and gathering information. Hanuman's journey to Lanka represents a profound lesson in the art of communication—understanding the audience, delivering messages with clarity and compassion, and listening to the feedback received. This dual aspect of communication is crucial in leadership, where the flow of information must be both ways.

Moreover, Hanuman's return to Rama, after successfully locating Sita and delivering the message, is a testament to his reliability and the trust Rama places in him. This trust is fundamental to effective leadership and teamwork. A leader must inspire trust through consistent and transparent communication, ensuring that team members feel valued and understood.

## Responsibility in Leadership

Another significant aspect of Hanuman's role as a messenger is his sense of responsibility. Being a messenger for a figure like Rama comes with immense responsibilities—accurately conveying messages, interpreting the intentions and emotions behind them, and managing the reactions of the recipients. Hanuman's execution of these tasks without error highlights the depth of his commitment and his understanding of the gravity of his role.

The responsibility of a leader, therefore, extends beyond mere task execution. It involves bearing the weight of expectations, the outcomes of decisions, and the well-being of followers. Hanuman's actions as a messenger illustrate how leaders must handle responsibilities with care, ensuring that their decisions and actions lead to positive outcomes for their teams and the wider community.

**Integrity and Accountability**

A crucial part of handling responsibility is maintaining integrity and being accountable for one's actions. Hanuman's journey not only shows his commitment to completing the tasks assigned to him but also his readiness to face any consequences. His approach to Sita, his interactions with her, and his conduct in the enemy's territory all reflect a deep sense of duty and an unwavering moral compass.

In modern leadership contexts, this translates to leaders being accountable for not only their successes but also their failures. Learning from mistakes, being transparent about challenges, and being open to feedback are all aspects of accountability that build trust and credibility in leadership roles.

**Implications for Modern Leadership**

Hanuman as the messenger offers numerous lessons for contemporary leaders. His story encourages leaders to be effective communicators, responsible handlers of tasks, and individuals of integrity. Emulating Hanuman's approach can lead to more empathetic, effective, and ethical leadership. Leaders can create environments where communication flows freely, where responsibility is embraced, and where integrity guides decisions.

By following in Hanuman's footsteps, leaders not only fulfill their roles more effectively but also inspire their teams to higher levels of performance and satisfaction. In essence, the role of Hanuman as a messenger in the "Hanuman Chalisa" is not just a portrayal of a mythological figure's duties but a timeless guideline on the virtues of good communication and responsible leadership.

༄༄༄

## 5: The Protector

In verses 9 and 10, Hanuman is revered as a powerful protector, shielding his devotees from harm. His protective nature is not only physical but also spiritual, providing a sense of safety that is deeply comforting to those who pray to him. This role as a protector emphasizes the broader theme of divine guardianship, where deities play an active role in safeguarding their followers.

**Verses 9-10:** His power to ward off evil and protect devotees.

Explores themes of protection, safety, and the role of divine intervention in human affairs.

ᐅᐅᐅ

# FIVE

# THE PROTECTOR

In verses 9 and 10 of the "Hanuman Chalisa," Hanuman is revered not only for his strength and devotion but also for his role as a protector. These verses focus on his abilities to ward off evil and safeguard devotees, highlighting a fundamental aspect of his divine nature. Hanuman's role as a protector is deeply embedded in his narratives, where he consistently intervenes to ensure the safety and well-being of those he serves, particularly Lord Rama and his allies. This protective aspect not only underscores the powers attributed to Hanuman but also reflects broader themes of protection, safety, and divine intervention in human affairs.

**Hanuman as a Symbol of Protection**

Hanuman is often depicted in mythology as a guardian and a savior, who is called upon in times of danger and distress. His actions, as described in various stories, paint him as a formidable force against all forms of evil and adversity. The "Hanuman Chalisa" reinforces this depiction, offering prayers that remind believers of the safety and security that Hanuman's presence provides. It is believed that chanting these verses can invoke Hanuman's protection, shielding the chanter from harm and warding off negative influences.

This belief in Hanuman's protective powers is not just a testament to his divine attributes but also a reflection of the human need for safety and assurance in a precarious world. Devotees turn to Hanuman as a source of comfort and strength, seeking his divine intervention during personal crises or community-wide difficulties. His role transcends the physical, encompassing the emotional and spiritual realms, offering a shelter that is both tangible and metaphysical.

## The Role of Divine Intervention

The concept of divine intervention, as exemplified by Hanuman's protective role, plays a significant role in the lives of many believers. This intervention is often seen as a guiding force that not only prevents physical dangers but also aids in making moral choices and pursuing the path of righteousness. Hanuman's interventions are thus viewed not merely as acts of saving grace but also as lessons in virtuous living and ethical decision-making.

In many stories, Hanuman intervenes at critical moments to guide and protect characters who strive to uphold dharma (moral and righteous duty). His involvement is therefore not just protective but also educative, teaching both direct beneficiaries and onlookers about the values of courage, fidelity, and selfless service. These narratives encourage individuals to reflect on the larger role of divine forces in their lives, acknowledging that spiritual growth often comes with challenges that require both divine and personal resolution.

## Protection in a Modern Context

While the idea of divine protection may seem anchored in ancient spirituality, its relevance extends into modern times, addressing contemporary needs for security and support in a rapidly changing world. In today's world, where uncertainties and anxieties loom large, the protector role of Hanuman can be interpreted as a metaphor for finding inner strength and resilience.

Embodying Hanuman's protective spirit, individuals are encouraged to develop their capacities to safeguard themselves and others, whether through physical means, mental toughness, or spiritual faith. This approach to protection emphasizes the importance of community, cooperation, and mutual support—qualities that Hanuman demonstrated through his actions.

**Implications for Personal Growth and Community Well-being**

Beyond personal protection, Hanuman's role as a protector has implications for community well-being. It highlights the importance of being vigilant and prepared, qualities necessary for any community leader or protector. Just as Hanuman was ready to face any danger to safeguard Dharma and his devotees, people today can draw upon his example to foster safer, more supportive environments in their own communities.

Moreover, understanding Hanuman's protective role encourages a proactive stance towards personal and collective security. It suggests that protection is not just about warding off external threats but also about building internal strengths and capabilities. Thus, by fostering qualities such as vigilance, resilience, and mutual care, communities can not only defend but also empower themselves, mirroring Hanuman's balanced approach to protection and service.

The portrayal of Hanuman as a protector in the "Hanuman Chalisa" offers rich insights into the themes of protection, safety, and divine intervention. These concepts, deeply rooted in mythological narratives, continue to resonate with modern audiences, offering spiritual and practical guidance for overcoming adversity and enhancing personal and community well-being. Through his example, Hanuman inspires a comprehensive approach to protection that encompasses physical safety, moral integrity, and spiritual fortitude.

ᎶᎶᎶ

### *6: The Embodiment of Victory*

*Verses 11 and 12 depict Hanuman as a symbol of victory, providing assurances of success to his devotees through his divine intervention. This embodiment of victory is not just about conquering enemies but also about overcoming personal limitations and obstacles, inspiring believers to pursue their goals with confidence and divine support.*

***Verses 11-12:*** *Hanuman's assurance of success.*

*Discusses how faith and perseverance lead to success, using Hanuman as a symbol of victory against odds.*

༁༁༁

# SIX

# THE EMBODIMENT OF VICTORY

Verses 11 and 12 of the "Hanuman Chalisa" depict Hanuman as the embodiment of victory, highlighting his assurance of success to those who seek his guidance and protection. These verses not only celebrate Hanuman's triumphs in various episodes of the Ramayana but also symbolize the universal themes of overcoming adversity through faith and perseverance. Hanuman's narrative provides a powerful metaphor for victory against odds, serving as a beacon of hope and resilience for his devotees and followers.

**Hanuman as a Symbol of Victory**

Hanuman's many feats, from his leap across the ocean to his role in the battle of Lanka, are legendary and depict him as a figure capable of overcoming insurmountable challenges. These stories are not just tales of adventure and courage; they are testimonies to his unwavering dedication to Lord Rama and his cause. This dedication is intricately linked to his victories, suggesting that success is not merely a result of strength or might but is deeply rooted in loyalty, faith, and the perseverance to pursue righteousness.

The verses in the "Hanuman Chalisa" that focus on his assurance of success reinforce this message. They encourage devotees to look to Hanuman as a source of inspiration when faced with their challenges. The narrative promotes an understanding that victory is attainable not just through divine intervention but through the emulation of Hanuman's virtues—his strength, courage, wisdom, and unwavering commitment to duty.

## Faith and Perseverance as Pathways to Success

The story of Hanuman is a vivid illustration of how faith and perseverance can lead to success. Hanuman's faith in Rama and his divine mission powered his actions, enabling him to perform feats that would seem impossible to ordinary beings. This faith was complemented by his perseverance—despite the obstacles and setbacks he faced, his resolve did not waver, and his actions were consistent and purposeful.

In personal and professional life, these principles translate into a powerful formula for overcoming obstacles. Faith—whether in a higher power, in oneself, or in the righteousness of one's path—provides the moral and emotional support necessary to pursue one's goals. Perseverance, or the relentless pursuit of an objective despite difficulties, ensures that one remains steadfast and focused, driving towards success even when immediate results are not evident.

## Implementing Hanuman's Lessons in Modern Contexts

Implementing the lessons from Hanuman's life into modern-day challenges requires an understanding that real victories are often the result of continued effort and moral integrity. In a world that frequently values immediate gratification and success, Hanuman's example is a reminder of the importance of the long-term view—acknowledging that worthwhile achievements require time, patience, and persistent effort.

For individuals facing personal challenges, Hanuman's story is a source of comfort and motivation. It teaches that setbacks are natural but can be overcome with faith and persistence. For professionals, these lessons underline the importance of ethical conduct, dedication to one's duties, and the courage to stand by one's principles, even in adverse conditions.

Furthermore, in leadership roles, the embodiment of victory as portrayed through Hanuman's character provides insights into leading with integrity. Leaders who embody the qualities of Hanuman—strength, wisdom, humility, and a focus on the greater good—are more likely to inspire their teams, overcome organizational challenges, and achieve sustainable success.

**The Broader Implications of Victory**

The concept of victory extends beyond personal or professional success. It also involves the triumph of good over evil, of ethical values over corruption, and of truth over deceit. Hanuman's victories are not celebrated because they are his alone but because they represent the victory of divine will and righteousness over chaos and disorder.

Thus, Hanuman as the embodiment of victory inspires not just the pursuit of personal goals but also the pursuit of a higher, collective good. His life encourages individuals and communities to strive for a world where integrity, duty, and justice prevail. In this way, the victory that Hanuman represents is not just about overcoming external challenges but also about achieving inner growth and societal harmony.

In essence, Hanuman's role as the embodiment of victory in the "Hanuman Chalisa" offers profound insights into achieving success through faith and perseverance. It encourages individuals to face life's battles with courage and integrity, holding onto the belief that righteous efforts are eventually met with success. Through his example, Hanuman continues to inspire a path of resilience and triumph, guiding countless individuals in their journeys through life's varied challenges.

ᎠᎠᎠ

### 7: The Guardian of Gateways

*Verses 13 and 14 elaborate on Hanuman's role as the guardian at the gates, metaphorically representing his position at the thresholds of important changes and decisions. His guardianship ensures safe passage through life's transitions, offering both protection and blessings. This role highlights the importance of guardianship in navigating the critical junctures of one's life journey.*

*Verses 13-14: Hanuman guarding the gates and empowering the gates of the fortress.*

*Examines the metaphor of gates as life's transitions and the role of guardianship in personal growth.*

༓༓༓

# SEVEN

# THE GUARDIAN OF GATEWAYS

Verses 13 and 14 of the "Hanuman Chalisa" explore Hanuman's role as the guardian of gateways, a position that involves more than just physical protection; it encompasses the spiritual and metaphorical guarding of transitional spaces in life. This role aligns Hanuman not only as a protector but also as a guide and facilitator through life's various gateways—critical junctures where significant changes occur. The metaphor of gates is rich in symbolic meaning, suggesting both opportunities and challenges, and Hanuman's guardianship offers insights into how individuals might navigate these pivotal moments with grace and wisdom.

## Guardianship as a Spiritual Endeavor

Hanuman's guardianship at the gates of the fortress, where he stood as a sentinel, symbolizes his role in overseeing critical thresholds in the epic tales. Such thresholds are not merely physical entry points but are emblematic of significant life transitions and transformative periods. In spiritual terms, guardians at the gates are often seen as figures who grant passage into new realms of experience and understanding, guiding souls as they transition from one phase of existence to another. Hanuman, in this capacity, is not just guarding a physical space but is also safeguarding the spiritual welfare of those who pass through these gateways.

This representation offers a profound metaphor for personal growth. Each individual faces numerous 'gates' throughout their life—moments of decision that lead to new paths such as career changes, marriages, births, and even moments of profound personal realization. Hanuman's role as a guardian inspires a mindful approach to these transitions, encouraging a recognition of the potential for growth and transformation that such moments hold.

**Navigating Life's Transitions**

Navigating life's transitions effectively requires wisdom, courage, and discernment—qualities that Hanuman embodies. As the guardian of gateways, he offers an archetype for handling transitions with vigilance and integrity. This involves being aware of the challenges and opportunities each transition presents and making choices that align with one's deepest values and highest aspirations.

Moreover, Hanuman's guardianship implies an active engagement with these life transitions. Instead of passively experiencing changes, it suggests taking an active role in shaping the outcomes of these pivotal moments, much like Hanuman who not only protects but also empowers and blesses those who pass through the gates. This proactive approach to life's transitions is crucial for personal development, as it encourages individuals to take control of their journey, making conscious choices that lead to more fulfilling outcomes.

**The Role of Guardianship in Personal Growth**

Guardianship in personal growth pertains not only to self-guardianship but also to the role individuals might play in guiding others. Just as Hanuman protects and oversees the well-being of others, individuals can take on mentorship roles, guiding and protecting others through their transitional phases. This aspect of guardianship enhances one's own growth through the act of service, which enriches both the mentor and the mentee.

Such guardianship also extends to the guarding of ethical and moral values during times of change. Hanuman's unwavering commitment to dharma (duty and righteousness) despite numerous challenges is a lesson in maintaining integrity under pressure. This teaches that being a guardian of one's principles is as important as guiding physical and spiritual transitions. Upholding one's values in the face of adversity or during major life changes can define the quality of the outcome and the depth of personal growth achieved.

**Empowerment Through Guardianship**

Hanuman's empowering presence at the gates also suggests that true guardianship involves enabling others to find their strength and path. By empowering those he protects, Hanuman enhances their ability to manage their own transitions and to face their challenges with increased confidence and capability. This empowering aspect of guardianship is critical in any leadership or mentorship role, where the goal is not just to lead or instruct but to enable others to become self-reliant and resilient.

Guardianship, therefore, involves a balance between protection and empowerment, between guiding and enabling, and between maintaining safety and encouraging exploration. Hanuman's dual role as both protector and empowerer at the gates provides a powerful model for this balanced approach, showing that through wise and vigilant guardianship, individuals can navigate life's crucial gateways not just safely but also successfully.

In essence, the metaphor of Hanuman as the guardian of gateways in the "Hanuman Chalisa" offers valuable lessons on navigating life's transitions. It highlights the importance of being vigilant and proactive during periods of change, the value of guarding one's ethical values, and the significance of empowering oneself and others. Through this lens, Hanuman's guardianship becomes a guiding principle for personal and spiritual development, illuminating the path through the complex gateways of life.

☙☙☙

### *8: The Dispeller of Distress*

*In verses 15 and 16, Hanuman is hailed as the dispeller of distress, alleviating the sufferings of those who invoke his name. This capability extends beyond physical relief, encompassing spiritual and emotional solace as well. His intervention is a reminder of the power of faith and devotion to overcome life's adversities.*

**Verses 15-16**: *Removal of obstacles and distress.*

*Looks at overcoming obstacles through resilience, mirrored in Hanuman's role as a remover of impediments.*

ঌঌঌ

# EIGHT

## THE DISPELLER OF DISTRESS

Verses 15 and 16 of the "Hanuman Chalisa" celebrate Hanuman as the dispeller of distress, focusing on his revered capacity to remove obstacles and alleviate the sufferings of his devotees. This role is pivotal, not just in the mythological contexts of his actions in the Ramayana but also in how individuals today can draw on his example to manage and overcome the challenges in their own lives. Hanuman's ability to clear obstacles is deeply symbolic, suggesting not just physical removal but also the psychological and spiritual resilience required to overcome difficulties.

**Hanuman's Role as a Remover of Impediments**

In various stories recounted in Hindu scriptures, Hanuman is depicted overcoming formidable challenges with a blend of strength, wit, and devotion. These stories highlight his ability to confront and eliminate barriers, not just for himself but for the benefit of others, particularly to aid Rama and his allies. His actions are driven by a deep-seated desire to serve, a quality that elevates his interventions from mere acts of bravery to profound demonstrations of selfless service.

This role of Hanuman resonates strongly with the human condition, where life often presents various forms of obstacles—physical, emotional, or spiritual. His example provides a template for navigating these challenges, emphasizing that the power to overcome comes from a combination of inner strength, clarity of purpose, and the unwavering resolve to act for the good of all.

## Overcoming Obstacles through Resilience

The concept of resilience is central to understanding how obstacles can be overcome. Resilience is the ability to recover from difficulties, to spring back into shape, much like Hanuman does after facing down threats or setbacks. This quality is not an inherent trait but something that can be developed through experience and through embracing certain spiritual or psychological principles—principles that Hanuman embodies.

Resilience involves maintaining a positive outlook, adapting to circumstances, and continuing to move forward despite setbacks. Hanuman's journey is replete with instances where his resilience is put to the test—be it his leap across the ocean or his search through Lanka. Each scenario showcases not just his physical might but his mental fortitude and his ability to persevere through seemingly impossible odds.

## Spiritual Resilience and Faith

Hanuman's resilience is deeply intertwined with his faith. His unyielding devotion to Rama provides him with the strength and motivation to confront and dispel distress. This illustrates a significant lesson: faith—whether in a higher power, a cause, or oneself—can be a powerful driver of resilience. It can provide the psychological strength needed to face adversity and to channel one's energies constructively, even in the face of overwhelming odds.

In practical terms, this spiritual resilience can be cultivated through practices such as meditation, prayer, or other forms of spiritual engagement that reinforce one's values and beliefs. These practices not only enhance one's capacity to deal with immediate obstacles but also prepare one for future challenges, imbuing them with a sense of purpose and perspective that transcends immediate concerns.

## Empowerment through the Removal of Obstacles

Another crucial aspect of Hanuman's role as the dispeller of distress is the empowerment that comes from removing obstacles. When impediments are cleared, not only is the path ahead made clearer, but individuals are also provided with the opportunity to grow, to develop, and to achieve their potential. This empowerment is a natural consequence of overcoming challenges but is also a deliberate outcome of the support and intervention by figures like Hanuman.

In a broader sense, empowering others involves helping them to see and overcome their obstacles. Just as Hanuman aids those in distress, individuals can support each other through mentorship, guidance, and by providing practical help in times of need. This collaborative approach to overcoming obstacles can strengthen relationships, build communities, and foster a culture of mutual support and resilience.

## Integrating Hanuman's Lessons into Daily Life

Integrating the lessons from Hanuman's role as the dispeller of distress involves recognizing the obstacles in one's path and approaching them with courage, wisdom, and the support of one's faith and community. It requires an acknowledgment that life's challenges are not merely hurdles but opportunities for growth and self-improvement.

By embodying Hanuman's qualities—his strength, resilience, and his devotion—individuals can transform their approach to life's challenges. They can learn to see obstacles as chances to demonstrate their resolve and to strengthen their character, much like Hanuman does in his epic tales. This perspective not only helps in overcoming immediate difficulties but also in building a foundation of strength and resilience that benefits all aspects of life.

In essence, the depiction of Hanuman as the dispeller of distress in the "Hanuman Chalisa" serves as a profound reminder of the human capacity to overcome adversity through faith, resilience, and collective support. His example inspires individuals to face their challenges with courage and to assist others in their struggles, fostering a world where obstacles are seen not just as impediments but as catalysts for growth and empowerment.

ᐖᐖᐖ

### 9: Master of Senses

*Verses 17 and 18 focus on Hanuman's mastery over his senses, a testament to his self-control and spiritual discipline. This mastery allows him to perform his duties with exceptional focus and clarity, serving as an inspiration for followers to cultivate similar control over their desires and impulses to lead a more disciplined and focused life.*

**Verses 17-18:** *Hanuman's mastery over his senses.*

*Discusses self-control and mastery over desires and fears, reflecting on mindfulness and self-discipline.*

ᗰᗰᗰ

# NINE

## MASTER OF SENSES

Verses 17 and 18 of the "Hanuman Chalisa" highlight Hanuman's mastery over his senses, a vital aspect of his character that enhances his abilities and contributes to his effectiveness as a servant, warrior, and leader. This mastery is not just about physical restraint but encompasses a deep, philosophical approach to self-control, mindfulness, and self-discipline. Such control is crucial for anyone seeking to lead a balanced, ethical, and focused life, making Hanuman's example particularly relevant in today's fast-paced world.

**The Importance of Sensory Mastery**

Hanuman's mastery over his senses is a testament to his great spiritual achievements and his immense discipline. In many spiritual traditions, control over the senses is considered a fundamental step toward achieving higher states of consciousness and spiritual enlightenment. The senses often tie individuals to the material aspects of the world and can lead to distraction, temptation, and sometimes even moral downfall. By mastering these senses, Hanuman is able to focus his energies more effectively and act in accordance with his dharma (duty) without distraction.

This control over the senses allows Hanuman to undertake the incredible feats that are recounted in the Ramayana and other stories. Whether it is the leap to Lanka or his ability to shrink to the size of a thumb, these stories metaphorically reflect his mastery over the material world, including his physical form and desires. Such mastery is an integral part of his spiritual and worldly success, providing a stable foundation for his actions and decisions.

## Self-Control and Its Benefits

The practice of self-control as demonstrated by Hanuman involves more than just avoiding temptation; it is about cultivating a disciplined lifestyle that aligns with one's spiritual and ethical values. Self-control helps in maintaining focus, conserving energy, and prioritizing long-term goals over immediate gratifications. In the context of modern life, this can translate into better decision-making in areas such as finance, relationships, career, and personal health.

For instance, in the professional realm, self-control can help individuals manage their reactions to stressful situations, leading to more thoughtful communication and effective leadership. In personal life, it can mean better management of emotional responses and impulses, leading to healthier relationships and lifestyle choices.

## Mindfulness and Self-Discipline

Closely linked with self-control is the practice of mindfulness—being fully present and aware of one's thoughts, feelings, and actions. Hanuman's actions are always deliberate and aware, guided by deep mindfulness of his goals and the needs of those he serves. This mindfulness ensures that his actions are not just reactions to external stimuli but are well-considered responses to the situations at hand.

Self-discipline, a natural extension of self-control and mindfulness, involves setting rules and boundaries for oneself and adhering to them consistently. It is about creating habits that lead to effectiveness and satisfaction in life. Hanuman's life, marked by disciplined practices, including his devotion to Rama and his adherence to a life of service and celibacy, showcases the power of self-discipline in achieving one's purpose and maintaining ethical integrity.

## Integrating Mastery Over Senses in Daily Life

Integrating mastery over the senses into daily life involves regular practice and commitment. It can start with simple steps such as regular meditation, which helps in calming the mind and bringing awareness to the present moment. Practicing mindfulness in everyday activities, like eating, walking, or listening, can also cultivate a greater sense of control over the senses.

Furthermore, setting and adhering to a daily routine that aligns with one's values can enhance self-discipline. This could include dedicated times for work, exercise, study, and relaxation. Over time, these practices can help diminish the control that unchecked sensory inputs and desires have over one's life, leading to greater peace and effectiveness.

## The Broader Implications of Sensory Mastery

On a broader scale, mastery over the senses can lead to a more harmonious society. When individuals exercise control over their impulses and focus on mindful living, they are less likely to engage in behaviors that are harmful to themselves or others. This can reduce conflicts, increase productivity, and enhance the overall quality of life in communities.

Hanuman's example of sensory mastery provides valuable lessons on the importance of self-control, mindfulness, and discipline. By embodying these qualities, individuals can navigate life's challenges with greater ease and effectiveness, achieve their personal and professional goals, and contribute positively to the world around them. In essence, Hanuman's mastery over his senses not only underscores his spiritual greatness but also offers a practical and profound blueprint for personal development and societal well-being.

ᐅᐅᐅ

**10: The Formidable Force**

*Verses 19 and 20 explore Hanuman's formidable form, which encapsulates his divine strength and his intimidating presence that can dispel evil. This formidability is both a literal and symbolic representation of his immense power, serving as a deterrent to evil and an assurance of protection for the good.*

**Verses 19-20:** *Descriptions of Hanuman's formidable form.*

*Analyzes the significance of inner strength and the power of divine presence.*

ᗡᗡᗡ

# TEN

# THE FORMIDABLE FORCE

Verses 19 and 20 of the "Hanuman Chalisa" depict Hanuman in his most formidable form, a representation that encapsulates not only his immense physical strength but also his powerful spiritual presence. This imagery of Hanuman as a towering figure serves to highlight the profound blend of physical prowess and divine energy, underscoring a deeper narrative about the nature of true power and strength.

**The Dual Nature of Hanuman's Formidability**

Hanuman's formidability is expressed in two primary ways: through his physical might and through the spiritual aura that surrounds him. His physical capabilities are legendary; he is able to change size at will, fly vast distances, and lift entire mountains. These feats, while miraculous, are manifestations of his divine origin as a son of the wind god, Vayu. However, his formidability is not solely attributable to his physical abilities. It is equally a function of his spiritual power, which he derives from his unwavering devotion to Lord Rama and his deep adherence to the principles of dharma (righteousness).

This dual nature of strength—physical combined with spiritual—offers a more holistic understanding of what it means to be truly powerful. It suggests that real strength is more than just physical capabilities; it is equally about the moral and spiritual virtues one embodies. Hanuman's strength, therefore, is as much about his integrity, his courage, his selflessness, and his loyalty as it is about his supernatural feats.

**Inner Strength and Its Impact**

The concept of inner strength is pivotal in understanding Hanuman's role and his influence. Inner strength stems from a combination of self-discipline, ethical convictions, emotional resilience, and spiritual wisdom. Hanuman exemplifies these qualities consistently, whether he is undertaking Rama's mission, advising other characters in the epics, or dealing with adversaries. His inner strength allows him to face daunting challenges without faltering, making decisions that are aligned with the greater good rather than personal benefit.

This inner fortitude is particularly relevant in contemporary settings where ethical dilemmas and complex challenges frequently arise. Hanuman's example serves as a reminder that inner strength is essential for navigating such situations effectively. It provides the moral compass and the courage needed to act rightly, even when such actions are difficult or demanding.

**The Power of Divine Presence**

Hanuman's formidable form is also a manifestation of divine presence, which refers to the sense of a higher spiritual power that guides and energizes a person. In Hanuman's case, this divine presence is palpably linked to his devotion to Rama, which imbues him with extraordinary capabilities and profound serenity. This connection highlights the transformative power of faith and devotion, suggesting that spiritual alignment with a higher purpose or being can elevate an individual's capacities and impact.

The divine presence in Hanuman's life is not just a source of power but also a beacon of hope and assurance to others. His presence reassures the distressed, fortifies the fearful, and inspires the hopeless. Thus, the divine aspect of Hanuman's formidability provides not only personal strength but also communal support, uplifting those around him through spiritual and moral leadership.

**Integrating Lessons from Hanuman's Formidability**

Integrating the lessons from Hanuman's formidable nature into one's life involves recognizing and cultivating one's inner strengths and connecting with a higher spiritual or moral purpose. It means understanding that true strength involves a blend of physical, emotional, and spiritual elements and that developing each of these aspects is crucial for a well-rounded and impactful life.

For individuals, this might mean engaging in practices that enhance physical health and vitality, foster emotional resilience, and deepen spiritual understanding. For communities, it implies nurturing leaders and members who embody these qualities and who can contribute positively to the collective welfare.

Moreover, recognizing the power of divine presence—whether one interprets it religiously or more secularly as an alignment with universal values—can inspire individuals to live more purposefully and to strive for greater harmony and impact in their actions.

**The Broader Implications of Hanuman's Form**

Finally, the broader implications of Hanuman's formidable form resonate beyond individual and community levels to encompass societal norms and values. Societies that honor and cultivate both physical vigor and spiritual depth are likely to be more resilient, ethical, and harmonious. Hanuman's balanced embodiment of strength offers a model for such societies, suggesting that the truest form of power is holistic, inclusive, and morally grounded.

In essence, the depiction of Hanuman as a formidable force in the "Hanuman Chalisa" is not just a celebration of his mythical strength but a profound commentary on the nature of true power. His example encourages a reevaluation of what it means to be strong, urging a move towards a more integrated approach that values physical prowess, moral integrity, and spiritual depth equally. Through this lens, Hanuman's legacy continues to inspire and guide, offering timeless lessons on strength, leadership, and the pursuit of a balanced and purposeful life.

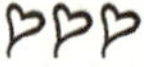

## 11: The Scholar

*In verses 21 and 22, Hanuman's deep knowledge of the scriptures and his intellectual capacity are highlighted, showcasing him as a scholar. This intellectual aspect is integral to his character, providing a balance between brawn and brain, and suggesting that true wisdom involves both learning and the practical application of knowledge.*

***Verses 21-22:*** *Hanuman's knowledge of scriptures and intellect.*

*Explores the power of education and knowledge, encouraging lifelong learning and intellectual growth.*

ᐅᐅᐅ

# ELEVEN

## THE SCHOLAR

Verses 21 and 22 of the "Hanuman Chalisa" highlight a less frequently discussed but equally vital aspect of Hanuman's character: his scholarship and profound intellect. These verses acknowledge his deep knowledge of the scriptures and his intellectual prowess, aspects that complement his physical strength and devotion. This scholarly side of Hanuman underscores the importance of education, knowledge, and intellectual engagement not just as ends in themselves, but as crucial components of a well-rounded, purposeful life.

**Hanuman as a Beacon of Intellectual Virtue**

Hanuman's role as a scholar is an integral part of his legacy, illustrating that true wisdom and learning are as important as physical might or spiritual devotion. This perspective is particularly significant given Hanuman's other well-known attributes such as strength and valor. It suggests that intellectual development is not just for the academically inclined but is crucial for everyone, including those who are more physically or spiritually oriented.

In the epic Ramayana, Hanuman demonstrates his intellectual capabilities in many instances, such as when he counsels Lord Rama or navigates complex situations with tact and diplomacy. His ability to chant the scriptures, converse with scholars, and strategize in battles highlights that knowledge and intellect are powerful tools in both worldly and spiritual endeavors.

## The Power of Education and Knowledge

The emphasis on Hanuman's knowledge of the scriptures brings to light the broader value of education. Education, in this context, is not merely the acquisition of factual information but the development of deeper understanding and wisdom. It involves a transformative process that refines a person's thoughts, ethics, and actions. Education empowers individuals, enabling them to make informed decisions, solve problems effectively, and contribute positively to society.

Moreover, knowledge as depicted through Hanuman's life is shown to be a foundation for effective leadership and governance. His decisions and actions, informed by his vast understanding of the Dharmic (righteous) laws and scriptures, are examples of how education can lead to just and moral leadership.

## Encouraging Lifelong Learning

The portrayal of Hanuman as a scholar also serves as a potent reminder of the importance of lifelong learning. Hanuman's learning was not limited to his early years but was a continuous part of his journey. This aspect of his character encourages individuals to view education as a lifelong pursuit rather than a finite goal. The modern world, with its ever-evolving technologies and rapidly changing socio-economic landscapes, particularly requires this continuous engagement with learning to navigate its complexities successfully.

Lifelong learning involves constantly updating one's knowledge and skills, staying curious about the world, and being open to new ideas.

This can be achieved through formal education, self-study, or through more informal means such as travel, cultural exchange, or practical experience. By fostering a habit of lifelong learning, individuals can adapt to changes more effectively and seize opportunities more readily.

## Intellectual Growth and Spiritual Enlightenment

Interestingly, Hanuman's intellectual pursuits also intersect with his spiritual quests. His profound understanding of the scriptures and his meditative practices are intrinsically linked, suggesting that intellectual growth and spiritual enlightenment are complementary pursuits. This connection highlights that true understanding is holistic, encompassing both the intellectual and the spiritual dimensions of life.

This holistic approach to knowledge and wisdom is particularly relevant in today's globalized world, where understanding diverse perspectives and cultures is crucial for peace and cooperation. Intellectual growth, therefore, can and should involve a deepening of spiritual and ethical understanding, which in turn fosters a more compassionate and tolerant worldview.

## Integrating Hanuman's Intellectual Legacy into Modern Life

Embracing Hanuman's legacy of scholarship involves more than valuing academic achievement; it is about nurturing a deep respect for knowledge and wisdom in all their forms. This includes encouraging critical thinking, fostering a love for learning, and promoting ethical reasoning in educational systems. It also means creating environments—at home, in schools, and in the workplace—that stimulate intellectual curiosity and allow for the free exchange of ideas.

Moreover, integrating this aspect of Hanuman's character into personal life involves adopting a mindset that values and seeks out learning in all interactions and experiences. Whether through reading, discussion, travel, or reflection, every situation offers opportunities for learning and intellectual growth.

In essence, Hanuman's portrayal as a scholar in the "Hanuman Chalisa" is a profound reminder of the enriching power of education and knowledge. His example inspires a balanced approach to life, where physical strength, spiritual devotion, and intellectual prowess are all seen as crucial for a fulfilled and effective existence. Through this multifaceted legacy, Hanuman continues to inspire individuals to pursue knowledge, think deeply, and live wisely, contributing to a more enlightened and thoughtful world.

### 12: *The Humble Servant*

*Verses 23 and 24 depict Hanuman as the epitome of humility and service, dedicated entirely to Lord Rama. His humility is not a sign of weakness but a reflection of his great strength and devotion, teaching us the value of serving others with a humble spirit.*

**Verses 23-24:** *His humility and service to Lord Rama.*

*Reflects on humility and service as core elements of leadership and personal integrity.*

ﻌﻌﻌ

# TWELVE

## THE HUMBLE SERVANT

Verses 23 and 24 of the "Hanuman Chalisa" delve into Hanuman's profound humility and his unwavering service to Lord Rama, portraying him as the epitome of servitude and selflessness. These verses celebrate his role not just as a devotee but as a servant whose actions are guided by devotion and a deep sense of duty. This humility, coupled with his commitment to service, provides a rich narrative exploring how these virtues underpin true leadership and personal integrity.

**The Essence of Hanuman's Humility**

Humility is one of the most defining characteristics of Hanuman. Despite his divine powers and his pivotal role in the epic Ramayana, he remains a figure who does not seek praise or glory for himself. His actions are motivated purely by the desire to serve Rama and ensure his well-being and success. This humility is not born out of weakness or fear but from a profound spiritual understanding and respect for life and duty. It is a humility that enhances his greatness, making his strength and wisdom accessible and beneficial to all those around him, rather than a means for personal aggrandizement.

This aspect of Hanuman's character is a powerful reflection on the role of ego in human interactions and achievements. By choosing humility, Hanuman demonstrates that true strength lies in knowing one's abilities and using them for a purpose greater than oneself. It teaches that leadership and influence are best exercised when they are rooted in the welfare of others rather than in the pursuit of personal power.

## Service as a Form of Devotion

Service, for Hanuman, is an extension of his devotion to Lord Rama and is the practical expression of his humility. His life is a testament to the idea that service to others is one of the highest forms of spiritual practice. This service is not passive but active, involving courage, initiative, and sometimes great personal risk. Hanuman's journey to Lanka, his battles in the war against Ravana, and his countless acts to protect Rama's allies are all driven by a commitment to service.

The notion that service forms the backbone of ethical leadership and personal integrity is profoundly relevant today. In a world often driven by individualism and competition, the values of cooperation, altruism, and selflessness stand out as pillars for sustainable and harmonious living. Leaders, much like Hanuman, can inspire loyalty and achieve great things when they prioritize the needs and well-being of their people over their desires.

## Humility and Service in Modern Leadership

The qualities of humility and service are essential for modern leadership. They foster environments where trust, respect, and loyalty flourish. Leaders who exhibit genuine humility are more approachable and relatable, making them more effective in their roles. They are likely to inspire their teams to greater commitment and effort, not through coercion but through example.

Furthermore, service-oriented leadership promotes a culture where the goals of the organization or community are aligned with the welfare of its members. This approach can transform workplaces and societies, making them more inclusive, supportive, and focused on mutual growth. In such environments, the success of the leader is directly connected to the success of their people, creating a powerful incentive for ethical behavior and selfless action.

**Integrating Humility and Service into Personal Life**

Incorporating humility and service into one's personal life involves recognizing and acknowledging the contributions of others, and putting the needs of others often before one's own desires. It requires an openness to learn from everyone and a commitment to contribute positively to the lives of others. Practicing humility might involve stepping back to let others shine, admitting when one is wrong, or being open to new ideas and perspectives.

Service can be integrated into everyday life by actively looking for ways to help others, whether in small acts of kindness, volunteering, or in one's professional duties. It involves making an effort to understand and address the needs of others, and using one's skills and resources to improve their situations.

**The Broader Impact of Humility and Service**

Embracing humility and service has a ripple effect, extending beyond individual benefits to impact broader societal structures. Societies where these values are cherished tend to be more resilient, compassionate, and peaceful. They are better equipped to handle internal conflicts and external pressures, as their members are committed to mutual support and understanding.

In essence, the portrayal of Hanuman as a humble servant in the "Hanuman Chalisa" offers profound insights into the virtues of humility and service. These qualities, while often overlooked in favor of more aggressive traits associated with leadership and success, are actually fundamental to true effectiveness and integrity. Hanuman's example serves as a guiding light for anyone seeking to lead a meaningful life, marked by respect for others and a commitment to the greater good.

ᗧᗧᗧ

## 13: The Healer

*Verses 25 and 26 focus on Hanuman's role as a healer, not just of physical ailments but of spiritual and emotional wounds as well. This healing is deeply tied to his spiritual powers, which bring comfort and recovery to those in need, emphasizing the holistic nature of healing that encompasses body, mind, and spirit.*

**Verses 25-26:** *Hanuman's role in healing and medicine.*

*Discusses the healing power of faith and spirituality in physical and emotional wellness.*

ᗑᗑᗑ

# THIRTEEN
## THE HEALER

Verses 25 and 26 of the "Hanuman Chalisa" shed light on another profound aspect of Hanuman's capabilities: his role as a healer. This role encompasses more than the physical act of healing; it extends to spiritual and emotional restoration. Hanuman's healing abilities are not just miraculous interventions but are deeply rooted in his spiritual power and his faith. These verses thus open up a broader discussion on the intrinsic link between faith, spirituality, and wellness, highlighting how these elements contribute to comprehensive healing processes.

**Hanuman's Healing Abilities**

In the epic narrative of the Ramayana, one of the most notable acts of healing performed by Hanuman is when he retrieves the Sanjeevani herb to revive Lakshmana, who was critically wounded in battle. This act is not only a demonstration of his dedication and bravery but also underscores his deep knowledge of Ayurvedic medicine. However, Hanuman's healing powers go beyond this single act. Throughout the epic, his presence itself is therapeutic, bringing comfort and courage to those in distress. His words and actions consistently soothe troubled minds, bolster wavering spirits, and instill hope and strength in his allies.

This multifaceted healing role makes Hanuman an emblematic figure of the healer who integrates physical, mental, and spiritual remedies. His approach is holistic, recognizing that true healing often requires attention to both the body and the soul.

## The Healing Power of Faith and Spirituality

The narrative of Hanuman as a healer brings to light the potent role of faith and spirituality in healing. Faith, in particular, is a powerful therapeutic tool; it provides individuals with the psychological strength needed to endure pain and suffering and to maintain hope even in dire circumstances. For many, faith in a higher power or in the spiritual laws of the universe offers a form of solace that physical remedies cannot provide.

Spirituality, encompassing practices that connect individuals to a higher sense of purpose and existence, also plays a crucial role in emotional and psychological healing. Practices such as meditation, prayer, and spiritual communion can significantly reduce stress, anxiety, and depression, leading to improved mental health and emotional resilience. Moreover, these practices often encourage a lifestyle that supports physical health, including habits related to diet, physical activity, and mindfulness.

## Integrating Spirituality into Modern Healing Practices

Incorporating spirituality into modern healing practices can greatly enhance the efficacy of conventional medical treatments. This integration involves recognizing the patient as a whole being who requires support on multiple levels, including the physical, emotional, and spiritual. Hospitals and healthcare providers increasingly acknowledge this holistic approach, integrating chaplaincy services, meditation programs, and therapy that incorporates spiritual counseling as part of comprehensive care.

Moreover, many traditional healing systems, such as Ayurveda, which Hanuman is indirectly associated with through the Sanjeevani herb, inherently combine physical treatments with spiritual practices. These systems offer valuable insights into how modern medicine might incorporate more holistic approaches to health and wellness.

## The Role of Healers in Society

Hanuman's example also illuminates the role of healers in society. Healers, whether they are medical professionals, spiritual leaders, or practitioners of traditional medicine, serve not only to treat illnesses but also to maintain the well-being of the community. They are often seen as custodians of both physical and spiritual health, guiding individuals through the challenges of life and aiding in the maintenance of societal harmony.

The effectiveness of healers can be significantly enhanced by qualities exemplified by Hanuman—compassion, dedication, and a deep-seated desire to serve others. These qualities ensure that the act of healing transcends the mere application of medical skills and becomes a profound service to humanity.

## Personal and Community Wellness

Embracing the healing principles demonstrated by Hanuman can contribute to personal and community wellness. On a personal level, integrating faith and spirituality into one's lifestyle can help manage stress, enhance life satisfaction, and foster overall well-being. On a community level, promoting these values can lead to a more supportive, empathetic, and cohesive society. This is particularly relevant in times of crisis or illness, where the communal sharing of spiritual practices and supportive networks can play a critical role in recovery and resilience.

In essence, Hanuman as a healer embodies the profound connection between faith, spirituality, and wellness. His example encourages a more integrated approach to healing—one that recognizes the interdependence of the body, mind, and spirit. By fostering these dimensions of health, individuals and societies can achieve a more balanced and fulfilling existence, reflecting the holistic health ideals epitomized by Hanuman's life and deeds.

### 14: The Bringer of Prosperity

*In verses 27 and 28, Hanuman is described as a bringer of prosperity, highlighting his ability to bless his devotees with both material abundance and spiritual wealth. This dual aspect of prosperity underlines the concept that spiritual richness often precedes material gain, and that true abundance includes emotional and spiritual fulfillment.*

**Verses 27-28:** *Hanuman's ability to bestow prosperity and pleasure.*

*Links spirituality with material and emotional prosperity, discussing how spiritual practices enhance life quality.*

༺༺༺

# FOURTEEN

## THE BRINGER OF PROSPERITY

Verses 27 and 28 of the "Hanuman Chalisa" celebrate Hanuman not only as a spiritual guide and protector but also as a bringer of prosperity and pleasure. These verses encapsulate the belief that Hanuman has the ability to influence both the material and emotional well-being of his devotees. This role highlights a broader, often overlooked aspect of spirituality—its capacity to enhance the quality of life by intertwining spiritual wellness with material and emotional prosperity.

**Spirituality and Material Prosperity**

The connection between spirituality and material prosperity is rooted in the idea that spiritual practices can lead to a more balanced and focused life, which in turn can enhance one's ability to succeed in material pursuits. Hanuman, as a divine entity, is believed to bestow blessings that can lead to material abundance for his followers. However, the deeper implication is that his spiritual guidance helps devotees cultivate qualities such as diligence, perseverance, and ethical behavior, which are essential for material success.

In many traditional cultures, prosperity is often viewed not merely in terms of wealth but as an overall well-being that includes a harmonious family life, career success, and financial stability—all outcomes that are thought to be fostered by a strong spiritual foundation. Hanuman's role as a bringer of prosperity thus highlights the belief that spiritual health is intrinsically linked to material success, suggesting that spiritual practices can foster an environment where material goals are achieved more readily.

**Emotional Prosperity Through Spiritual Practice**

Beyond material wealth, Hanuman's blessings are also seen as key to emotional prosperity. Emotional prosperity refers to feelings of happiness, contentment, and fulfillment that arise from a balanced and harmonious inner life. Spiritual practices, such as meditation, prayer, and the chanting of hymns like the "Hanuman Chalisa" itself, are tools that help manage stress, alleviate anxiety, and foster a deep sense of peace and contentment.

These practices encourage individuals to reflect on their lives, reassess their priorities, and focus on what truly matters, leading to a more fulfilled and joyous existence. The calm and clarity gained from regular spiritual practice allow individuals to handle daily challenges more effectively, maintain healthier relationships, and live in a state of gratitude and joy, all of which contribute to emotional prosperity.

**Spiritual Practices Enhancing Life Quality**

The enhancement of life quality through spiritual practices can be seen in various dimensions of life. For instance, individuals who engage in regular spiritual practices often report higher levels of life satisfaction and personal well-being. These practices imbue their lives with a sense of purpose and meaning, which are fundamental to personal happiness and satisfaction.

Moreover, spirituality can foster community and belonging, which are vital for emotional health. Communities formed around spiritual practices provide social support, shared values, and a sense of belonging, all of which are crucial for emotional well-being. Hanuman's role in these communities—as a symbol of strength, loyalty, and protection—reinforces these bonds and enhances the collective welfare of the group.

## Integrating Spirituality for Prosperity in Modern Life

Incorporating spirituality into modern life as a means to enhance prosperity involves recognizing and nurturing the spiritual dimensions of everyday experiences. This can mean setting aside time for meditation, prayer, or other spiritual practices; it can also mean approaching work and interpersonal relationships with a spirit of service and ethical conduct, inspired by Hanuman's example.

Furthermore, acknowledging the role of spirituality in achieving a balanced life encourages individuals to seek prosperity not just through material achievements but through the cultivation of personal virtues and community values. This holistic approach to prosperity acknowledges that true wealth includes spiritual depth and emotional balance, not just material abundance.

## The Broader Impact of Spiritual Prosperity

Embracing the concept of spiritual prosperity, as exemplified by Hanuman's blessings, has the potential to transform not only individual lives but also entire communities. By fostering values such as integrity, generosity, and compassion, societies can create environments where both material and emotional prosperity are enhanced. This leads to communities where individuals are not only successful but also support each other's well-being and growth.

In essence, Hanuman as the bringer of prosperity illuminates the profound connection between spirituality and the various forms of prosperity—material, emotional, and communal. His example encourages a reevaluation of what constitutes true prosperity, advocating for a balanced life that values spiritual growth as a fundamental component of success and well-being. Through this perspective, Hanuman continues to inspire a path that seeks not just individual achievement but the holistic flourishing of all aspects of life.

ᐅᐅᐅ

### 15: The Savior from Adversities

Verses 29 and 30 portray Hanuman as a savior who rescues his followers from adverse situations. This role is deeply spiritual, reflecting his divine ability to alter destinies and provide support during critical times. His presence is a source of reassurance that no matter the hardships, divine help is always at hand.

**Verses 29-30:** Deliverance from adverse fate.

Explores coping mechanisms in face of adversity, inspired by Hanuman's protection.

ᗡᗡᗡ

# FIFTEEN

# THE SAVIOR FROM ADVERSITIES

Verses 29 and 30 of the "Hanuman Chalisa" depict Hanuman as a savior from adversities, a divine protector who delivers his followers from difficult fates. This portrayal not only underscores his role as a guardian but also highlights the deeper spiritual and psychological mechanisms that enable individuals to cope with and overcome adversities. Through Hanuman's divine protection, devotees are inspired to develop resilience, find inner strength, and cultivate a mindset that views challenges as opportunities for growth and learning.

**Hanuman's Role in Overcoming Adversity**

Hanuman is revered not only for his physical strength and bravery but also for his ability to protect those in distress. His interventions are often crucial in moments of crisis, where his actions directly change the course of events for the better. However, the protection Hanuman offers extends beyond physical interventions; it also encompasses the spiritual strength and courage he instills in his devotees. This dual approach—direct intervention and empowerment—illustrates a comprehensive strategy for dealing with adversities, combining external support with internal resilience.

## Spiritual Protection as a Coping Mechanism

The concept of spiritual protection involves more than the belief in a higher power's ability to intervene in one's life; it also includes the faith that this power can guide and sustain an individual through trials and tribulations. For many, Hanuman's protection is a source of comfort and strength that helps them navigate life's uncertainties. The faith in his protection provides a psychological buffer against despair and hopelessness, encouraging a more optimistic and proactive approach to life's challenges.

Practically, this spiritual support can manifest as increased resilience—the capacity to recover quickly from difficulties. It can also enhance an individual's ability to remain calm and composed under pressure, attributes that are crucial when confronting challenges. The invocation of Hanuman for protection, therefore, is not merely a plea for divine intervention but also a strategy for psychological and emotional fortification.

## Developing Resilience Inspired by Hanuman

Drawing inspiration from Hanuman's example, individuals can develop their resilience by adopting several key attitudes and behaviors. First, maintaining a positive outlook is essential. Hanuman's unwavering focus on his goals, despite the obstacles he faced, demonstrates the power of a positive mindset. Maintaining such optimism in the face of adversity can significantly impact one's ability to persist and overcome challenges.

Second, embracing flexibility and adaptability—qualities Hanuman exhibited by changing his form and strategy according to the situation—is vital. In modern life, being adaptable in the face of changing circumstances can help manage stress and reduce the adverse impacts of unexpected events.

Third, nurturing a strong sense of duty and commitment to others, as shown by Hanuman's devotion to Rama and his readiness to help those in need, fosters resilience by providing a clear purpose and motivation to overcome personal and collective challenges.

## Cultivating Inner Strength

Beyond resilience, cultivating inner strength is essential for dealing with adversities. This strength is derived from a combination of self-awareness, spiritual practices, and the development of personal virtues such as courage, patience, and perseverance. Engaging in regular spiritual practices like meditation, prayer, or chanting can help build this inner strength, creating a solid foundation that sustains individuals through tough times.

Moreover, Hanuman's teachings encourage looking inward for solutions and strength. By developing a deep connection with one's inner self and aligning with one's core values and ethics, individuals are better equipped to face external challenges. This inner alignment ensures that actions and decisions are guided by wisdom and integrity, key components of effective adversity management.

## Integrating Lessons from Hanuman's Protection in Daily Life

Integrating the lessons from Hanuman's role as a savior from adversities involves recognizing the importance of both external supports—such as community and relationships—and internal resources—such as faith, resilience, and inner strength. It also involves actively cultivating these resources before crises occur, preparing individuals to handle adversities more effectively when they arise.

Furthermore, Hanuman's example encourages a proactive

approach to life's challenges. Instead of being passive victims of circumstances, individuals are inspired to take active steps to change their situations, drawing on both spiritual guidance and personal capabilities to effect positive changes in their lives.

In essence, Hanuman as the savior from adversities exemplifies how combining spiritual faith with practical resilience strategies can profoundly impact one's ability to cope with and overcome life's challenges. His protection inspires not just passive reliance on divine intervention but active engagement in developing the personal and communal strengths necessary for overcoming adversities. Through this holistic approach, individuals are empowered to transform their trials into opportunities for growth, guided by the wisdom and strength epitomized by Hanuman's enduring legacy.

### 16: The Lord of Courage

*In verses 31 and 32, Hanuman is celebrated as a figure of immense courage, whose daring feats inspire bravery in his devotees. His courage is not reckless but is driven by purpose and devotion, encouraging us to face our fears and challenges with a brave heart.*

***Verses 31-32:** His embodiment of courage and adventure.*

*Encourages embracing courage in everyday life, drawing parallels with Hanuman's adventures.*

༓༓༓

# SIXTEEN

# THE LORD OF COURAGE

Verses 31 and 32 of the "Hanuman Chalisa" depict Hanuman as the embodiment of courage and adventure, highlighting his fearless endeavors and the valor with which he faced numerous challenges. This portrayal serves not only as a testament to his legendary heroism but also as a source of inspiration for individuals seeking to incorporate courage into their everyday lives. Hanuman's adventures, marked by bold actions and a pioneering spirit, offer valuable lessons on the virtues of courage, risk-taking, and leadership.

**Hanuman's Emblematic Courage**

Hanuman's courage is most vividly displayed in his audacious leap across the ocean to Lanka, a feat that symbolizes his willingness to undertake risks for the sake of duty and loyalty. This act, along with his numerous other ventures, including his confrontations in the court of Ravana and his efforts to save his allies, illustrates a profound level of bravery that goes beyond mere physical actions. It speaks to a deeper, moral courage – the courage to stand up for what is right, even in the face of overwhelming odds.

This type of courage is crucial not only in epic tales but also in modern life, where moral and ethical challenges frequently arise. Hanuman's example teaches that courage is not the absence of fear, but the determination to act in spite of it. It involves making difficult decisions, often under pressure, and sometimes in situations where the outcomes are uncertain.

## Courage in Everyday Life

Integrating courage into daily life can manifest in various forms, from tackling new challenges at work or in personal development to standing up for others' rights or speaking out against injustices. Hanuman's courage inspires individuals to confront their fears, whether they relate to career changes, personal goals, or interpersonal conflicts.

The spirit of adventure seen in Hanuman's journeys also encourages a mindset open to exploration and learning. It suggests that life should be approached as a series of adventures where risks are opportunities for growth. Adopting this adventurous spirit can lead to discovering new potentials, learning new skills, and gaining fresh insights—all of which contribute to a richer, more fulfilling life.

## Drawing Parallels with Hanuman's Adventures

The parallels between Hanuman's adventures and everyday challenges highlight the relevance of his courage in contemporary contexts. Just as Hanuman navigated unknown territories and faced daunting foes, individuals today encounter uncharted areas in their personal and professional lives that require them to venture beyond their comfort zones.

Drawing inspiration from Hanuman's adventures means recognizing that each challenge faced is an opportunity to demonstrate courage. This can be as simple as taking the initiative on a project, advocating for an unpopular but beneficial idea, or making a life change that aligns more closely with one's values despite societal pressures.

## Leadership and Courage

Courage is also an essential trait for effective leadership. Leaders who embody courage, like Hanuman, inspire confidence and respect from their followers. They are prepared to make tough decisions, guide others through crises, and envision transformative solutions. Hanuman's leadership during the battle in Lanka, where he rallied the vanara army and strategized their actions, underscores the importance of courageous leadership in achieving collective goals.

Leaders can cultivate this trait by practicing ethical decision-making, fostering transparency, and advocating for their team's welfare, even when these actions might be met with resistance or criticism. This form of courageous leadership not only achieves results but also builds a legacy of integrity and respect.

## Cultivating Courage through Spiritual Practice

Finally, Hanuman's life suggests that spiritual practices can strengthen one's inner courage. Regular engagement in practices such as meditation, prayer, or chanting can fortify the spirit and prepare individuals to face life's trials with a calm and focused mind. These practices help align personal actions with higher principles and provide the moral fortitude needed to act courageously in various situations.

In essence, the depiction of Hanuman as the Lord of Courage in the "Hanuman Chalisa" serves as a powerful reminder of the transformative impact of courage in one's life. His daring exploits and unwavering commitment to duty provide a blueprint for living courageously, urging individuals to rise above their limitations and embrace life's challenges with a brave heart. Through his example, Hanuman continues to inspire a fearless approach to both personal growth and community engagement, highlighting that true courage often leads to profound change and enrichment in life.

᭡᭡᭡

## 17: The Destroyer of Suffering

Verses 33 and 34 elaborate on Hanuman's capacity to alleviate suffering, positioning him as a divine force who not only understands pain but actively works to eliminate it. This role emphasizes his compassion and his proactive nature in removing obstacles that cause suffering, providing a model of empathy and action.

**Verses 33-34**: Hanuman's role in destroying suffering.

Focuses on overcoming suffering through spiritual growth and divine help.

𑗊𑗊𑗊

# SEVENTEEN

## THE DESTROYER OF SUFFERING

Verses 33 and 34 of the "Hanuman Chalisa" highlight Hanuman's significant role as the destroyer of suffering, underscoring his capacity to alleviate the hardships faced by his devotees through both his divine interventions and the spiritual guidance he provides. This depiction of Hanuman extends beyond the image of a warrior and protector to that of a compassionate deity who actively works to eradicate pain and anguish from the lives of his followers. The narrative surrounding Hanuman's role in this regard is deeply connected to the themes of spiritual growth and divine assistance, which are seen as vital mechanisms for overcoming life's various forms of suffering.

### Hanuman's Compassionate Interventions

Hanuman's interventions to relieve suffering are numerous and varied, ranging from physical healings, as seen when he carried the healing herb to revive Lakshmana, to more subtle forms of support, such as providing strength and courage to those in despair. His ability to sense and respond to the suffering of others is a testament to his deep empathy and boundless compassion. It is this compassionate nature that makes him a revered figure not only for his strength and valor but for his profound commitment to the welfare of all beings.

In the broader spiritual context, Hanuman's role as the destroyer of suffering reflects the Hindu belief in the power of divine forces to intervene in human affairs and alleviate the trials and tribulations of life. This belief is a source of immense comfort and hope for many, providing them with the strength to endure difficult times with the faith that divine help is always at hand.

**Spiritual Growth and Overcoming Suffering**

One of the primary ways in which Hanuman aids in destroying suffering is through promoting spiritual growth among his devotees. Spiritual growth involves the development of a deeper understanding of oneself and one's place in the cosmos, a process that often leads to greater inner peace and reduced personal suffering. The practices associated with spiritual growth—such as meditation, prayer, and the chanting of mantras—help individuals cultivate a state of mindfulness and serenity, which can alleviate mental and emotional suffering.

Moreover, spiritual growth encourages the cultivation of virtues such as patience, humility, and resilience, which are crucial for dealing with life's challenges. These virtues can transform an individual's approach to suffering, often changing their perception of and reaction to pain and adversity. By fostering a spiritual outlook, Hanuman guides his followers to view their struggles as opportunities for growth and enlightenment, thus reducing the impact of suffering on their lives.

**Divine Help in Alleviating Suffering**

The concept of divine help in alleviating suffering is central to Hanuman's role as a destroyer of suffering. Devotees often turn to

Hanuman for relief from pain and adversity, believing in his power to change their circumstances through divine intervention. This faith in divine help does not merely act as a psychological balm; it can lead to real changes in individuals' lives by inspiring them with the courage to take necessary actions or by opening up paths to solutions that were previously overlooked.

Divine help, as exemplified by Hanuman's interventions, also underscores the interconnectedness of the divine with the mundane. It suggests that the spiritual and the temporal are not separate but are intertwined aspects of existence, where changes in one can affect the other. Thus, spiritual solutions to suffering, facilitated by divine beings like Hanuman, are not merely about expecting miracles but about tapping into a deeper reality where spiritual forces actively influence the material world.

**Integrating Lessons from Hanuman's Life**

Integrating the lessons from Hanuman's life into dealing with personal suffering involves recognizing the power of faith, the importance of spiritual practices, and the value of divine guidance. Individuals can emulate Hanuman's example by striving to develop their spiritual lives, which in turn can provide them with the resources to combat suffering. This might involve regular spiritual disciplines, participating in community religious services, or engaging in acts of charity and compassion, all of which can enhance one's capacity to deal with pain and adversity.

Additionally, understanding and embracing the role of divine help can encourage individuals to remain hopeful and proactive in the face of suffering. It teaches that while divine help is a powerful aid, it often requires one to take practical steps towards alleviating one's own suffering. This balanced approach—between divine dependence and personal effort—is key to effectively overcoming the challenges and pains of life.

In essence, Hanuman as the destroyer of suffering offers a profound narrative on the possibilities of overcoming suffering through spiritual growth and divine assistance. His life and actions provide a powerful template for how individuals can address and mitigate the impacts of suffering in their lives, highlighting the transformative potential of spiritual development and compassionate living.

## 18: The Eternal Devotee

*Verses 35 and 36 highlight Hanuman's eternal devotion to Lord Rama, underscoring the timeless nature of his commitment. This devotion transcends the temporal bounds of the mythic narratives to offer contemporary lessons on the enduring power and relevance of unwavering loyalty and faith.*

***Verses 35-36:*** *Hanuman's eternal act of devotion.*

*Emphasizes the timeless nature of devotion and its place in the modern spiritual journey.*

# EIGHTEEN

## THE ETERNAL DEVOTEE

Verses 35 and 36 of the "Hanuman Chalisa" celebrate Hanuman as the eternal devotee, whose unwavering dedication to Lord Rama transcends time and continues to inspire countless generations. This portrayal emphasizes the enduring and timeless nature of true devotion, illustrating its profound impact not only on the devotee's spiritual journey but also on their ability to overcome life's adversities through spiritual growth and divine assistance.

**The Timeless Nature of Hanuman's Devotion**

Hanuman's devotion to Rama is legendary and serves as the cornerstone of his character. It is characterized by a depth of loyalty and love that goes beyond mere duty; it is a complete surrender of the self in service to another. This type of devotion is transformative, not just for the devotee but also for those who witness it. Hanuman's devotion is not confined to the historical or mythological context of the Ramayana; it continues to resonate through ages, offering lessons on the power and beauty of unconditional devotion.

In the context of modern spirituality, Hanuman's eternal act of devotion highlights the relevance of enduring spiritual commitments in an increasingly transient world. In an age where fleeting interests and momentary engagements are commonplace, the concept of lifelong or eternal devotion offers a counterpoint, emphasizing stability, depth, and persistence in spiritual pursuits. This form of devotion challenges individuals to look beyond the superficial and engage more deeply with their spiritual beliefs and practices.

## Devotion as a Pathway to Overcoming Suffering

Hanuman's devotion is also intimately connected with his role in alleviating suffering—both his own and that of others. His devotion provides him with the strength to face and overcome numerous challenges, from the search for Sita to the battles in Lanka. It is his commitment to Rama that imbues him with extraordinary capabilities and resilience, allowing him to perform feats that would otherwise be impossible.

For modern devotees, Hanuman's example illustrates how spiritual commitment can be a source of strength in times of adversity. Devotion can fortify the spirit against despair and can provide a sense of purpose and direction during difficult times. This is particularly relevant in a world where external circumstances can often be unpredictable and challenging. The internal anchor that devotion provides can help individuals navigate these challenges with greater equanimity and resilience.

## Integrating Devotion in Modern Spiritual Practices

Integrating the concept of eternal devotion into modern spiritual practices involves several key elements. First, it requires recognizing the value of long-term commitment in an age of distraction. This might mean dedicating oneself to regular spiritual practices such as meditation, prayer, or other forms of worship, despite the pressures and distractions of contemporary life.

Second, it involves deepening one's understanding of the object of devotion—whether it is a deity, a spiritual principle, or a set of values. This deepening understanding can help transform superficial beliefs into profound spiritual commitments, enhancing the devotee's spiritual growth and personal fulfillment.

Furthermore, devotion should also be expressed through actions. Just as Hanuman's devotion was demonstrated through his deeds, modern devotees are called to live out their spiritual commitments through acts of kindness, service, and ethical living. These actions reinforce the devotee's spiritual values and facilitate a tangible impact on their community and society.

**The Role of Devotion in Community and Society**

The impact of devotion extends beyond the individual to influence the broader community and society. Devotion promotes virtues such as selflessness, compassion, and altruism, which are essential for building cohesive and caring communities. In a society where individualism often prevails, the communal aspects of devotion can help foster a sense of connectedness and shared purpose.

Moreover, the example of an eternal devotee like Hanuman serves as a reminder of the enduring power of spiritual values in guiding human affairs. It challenges both individuals and communities to consider the long-term implications of their beliefs and actions, inspiring them to strive for a legacy of positive impact and spiritual integrity.

In essence, the depiction of Hanuman as the eternal devotee in the "Hanuman Chalisa" not only underscores the importance of devotion in the spiritual journey but also illustrates its transformative potential in overcoming adversity and fostering personal and communal well-being. Through his life, Hanuman exemplifies how timeless devotion can enrich the modern spiritual journey, providing a profound source of strength, guidance, and inspiration.

ᛈᛈᛈ

### 19: The Symbol of Hope

*In verses 37 and 38, Hanuman's depiction as a symbol of hope illustrates his role in lifting spirits and encouraging positive action among his followers. His character is a beacon of optimism, especially in times of despair, showing that with faith and perseverance, resurgence is always possible.*

**Verses 37-38**: *His role as a symbol of hope and inspiration.*

*Discusses how symbols like Hanuman inspire hope and motivate individuals toward greater good.*

ᗞᗞᗞ

# NINETEEN

## THE SYMBOL OF HOPE

Verses 37 and 38 of the "Hanuman Chalisa" illuminate Hanuman's role as a symbol of hope and inspiration. Throughout the ages, Hanuman has not only been revered as a deity with immense power but also as a beacon of hope for millions. His story and his deeds provide a profound source of motivation and encouragement for people facing challenges, reinforcing the belief that with faith, strength, and determination, any obstacle can be overcome.

**Hanuman as an Inspirational Figure**

Hanuman's actions in the Ramayana and his unwavering devotion and service to Lord Rama epitomize the virtues of courage, loyalty, and selflessness. These attributes make him a powerful symbol of hope, especially in times of difficulty. Whether it is his daring leap across the ocean to Lanka or his efforts to reunite Rama with Sita, Hanuman's adventures are filled with challenges that he overcomes with his strength and wit, providing a narrative thread that inspires resilience and optimism.

This depiction of Hanuman goes beyond the boundaries of mythology and enters the realm of personal and collective consciousness as a source of inspiration. For many, Hanuman is not just a character in an ancient epic but a living presence that influences their daily lives, offering comfort and encouragement. His story teaches that no challenge is too great when faced with virtue and determination.

## The Power of Symbols in Inspiring Hope

Symbols, such as Hanuman, play a crucial role in human culture and psychology. They encapsulate complex ideas and emotions and communicate these in a form that can be easily understood and felt. As a symbol of hope, Hanuman represents the human capacity to face adversity with courage and to remain steadfast in one's duties and commitments, even under the most trying circumstances.

Symbols like Hanuman also serve as anchors or focal points for communities. They provide a shared identity and a collective source of inspiration. In times of collective hardship, such symbols can unite people, giving them the strength to work together towards common goals. They remind individuals of their shared values and aspirations, motivating them towards actions that promote the greater good.

## Motivation Towards the Greater Good

The inspirational power of Hanuman encourages individuals not only to persevere through their personal trials but also to strive for the betterment of others. His life is a testament to the impact one can have when acting out of a sense of duty and compassion. This is particularly significant in the modern world, where actions driven by self-interest often dominate.

The story of Hanuman inspires people to look beyond their immediate concerns to the broader impacts of their actions on their community and the world at large. It promotes a sense of responsibility and encourages acts of kindness and public service. In this way, Hanuman as a symbol of hope is closely linked to the concept of karma in Hindu philosophy, which emphasizes the importance of performing righteous actions without attachment to outcomes.

## Integrating Hanuman's Inspirational Qualities in Daily Life

Integrating the qualities that Hanuman represents into daily life involves embracing virtues such as bravery, loyalty, and service. It requires individuals to act with integrity and to approach challenges with courage and optimism. Practically, this can mean standing up for what is right, offering help where it is needed, and maintaining a positive outlook even in the face of adversity.

Furthermore, reflecting on Hanuman's stories can be a form of meditation on the values he embodies. This reflection can provide spiritual nourishment and emotional resilience, reinforcing an individual's capacity to hope and aspire even when circumstances are daunting.

## The Enduring Legacy of Hope

In essence, Hanuman's role as a symbol of hope and inspiration speaks to his enduring legacy in the cultural and spiritual life of millions. His example transcends the mythological and becomes a part of the existential fabric that supports individuals and communities in their daily struggles and aspirations. By embodying the principles of courage, duty, and service, Hanuman continues to motivate people to rise above their limitations and to contribute to a world where hope, faith, and goodwill prevail. Through his stories and the values he represents, Hanuman remains a timeless symbol of hope, inspiring generations to strive for a higher purpose and to lead lives of greater meaning and impact.

ॐॐॐ

**20: *The Path to Liberation***

*The final verses, 39 and 40, culminate in the promise of liberation through devotion to Hanuman, linking spiritual practice to ultimate spiritual freedom. This assurance of moksha, or liberation, is not just a distant spiritual goal but a present possibility through dedicated practice and alignment with divine principles.*

***Verses 39-40:*** *Assurance of liberation through devotion to Hanuman.*

*Concludes by connecting the spiritual with the practical, offering insights on how devotion leads to personal and spiritual liberation.*

ᐅᐅᐅ

# TWENTY
## THE PATH TO LIBERATION

Verses 39 and 40 of the "Hanuman Chalisa" conclude with a profound assurance of liberation through devotion to Hanuman, encapsulating the essence of spiritual deliverance that Hanuman offers to his devotees. This section not only highlights the ultimate spiritual goal of moksha (liberation from the cycle of birth and death) but also ties it intricately to the practical applications of devotion in everyday life. The teachings emphasize how a life led in dedication to Hanuman, characterized by righteousness and service, can pave the way for both personal and spiritual freedom.

**Liberation Through Devotion**

The concept of liberation in Hindu philosophy is a profound and complex one, often seen as the ultimate aim of human life. Liberation is not merely about the cessation of physical existence but involves the soul's release from the shackles of worldly suffering and illusion. Devotion to Hanuman, as highlighted in these verses, is portrayed as a direct path to achieving this state. Hanuman himself is a symbol of perfect devotion and service, and his life exemplifies the virtues required to attain liberation.

Devotion to Hanuman involves more than ritual worship; it encompasses the emulation of his virtues—his strength, courage, humility, and unwavering commitment to the good. By aligning one's actions with these divine qualities, devotees can elevate their spiritual and moral character, moving closer to liberation. This alignment helps dissolve the ego, which in many spiritual traditions is considered the primary obstacle to liberation.

## The Practical Aspects of Devotion

While the ultimate goal of devotion may be spiritual liberation, it also has significant practical implications for daily life. Devotion as practiced through daily prayers, chants, and meditations on Hanuman can provide individuals with a sense of purpose and direction. It fosters a positive outlook, instills peace, and offers guidance in times of moral quandary or personal difficulty.

Furthermore, devotion to Hanuman encourages the practice of selflessness and service. Hanuman's legendary acts of service are not only spiritually uplifting but also inspire practical acts of kindness and generosity. These actions contribute to personal growth and societal well-being, reinforcing the social fabric and helping create a more compassionate community.

## Devotion as a Path to Personal Growth

Engaging in devotion to Hanuman is also a journey of personal transformation. It encourages the shedding of baser instincts such as greed, lust, and anger, and fosters the development of higher qualities such as compassion, bravery, and wisdom. This transformation is integral to the concept of liberation, which involves not just the soul's release from the cycle of birth and rebirth but also freedom from the negative tendencies that cause suffering in life.

The path of devotion is, therefore, both purifying and elevating, assisting devotees in transcending their limitations and embracing a higher state of consciousness. This personal elevation is a critical step towards achieving the freedom that comes with spiritual liberation, as it aligns the individual more closely with divine virtues.

## Connecting the Spiritual with the Practical

In essence, devotion to Hanuman serves as a bridge connecting the spiritual and the practical aspects of life. It offers a comprehensive approach to living that enhances the spiritual, moral, and social dimensions of existence. This holistic development is essential for liberation, as it ensures that spiritual progress is balanced with practical ethical living.

Moreover, the assurance of liberation through devotion to Hanuman offers hope and motivation, encouraging individuals to persist in their spiritual practices even in the face of life's challenges. It underscores the idea that every act of devotion, no matter how small, contributes to the soul's journey towards liberation.

## The Enduring Impact of Devotion

In conclusion, the verses of the "Hanuman Chalisa" that focus on liberation through devotion to Hanuman highlight a profound spiritual truth—that liberation is not an abstract concept but a tangible state that can be approached through daily acts of devotion, virtue, and service. Hanuman's life as a devout servant of Lord Rama and his role as a guide and protector offer a powerful template for living a life that balances spiritual aspirations with practical duties.

By following in Hanuman's footsteps, devotees can navigate the complexities of the world while keeping their sights set on the ultimate goal of liberation. This path, enriched by devotion and marked by righteous living, leads not only to personal fulfillment but also to the profound peace of spiritual freedom, offering a legacy of hope and inspiration for all who walk it.

ϟϟϟ

# Citation And References

*This book represents the culmination of extensive research and meticulous analysis, incorporating a diverse range of sources, including numerous books, scholarly studies, and personal experiences. Additionally, I have scoured various websites to gather relevant information and data essential for the compilation of this work. I have taken every precaution to ensure the accuracy of the information presented and have diligently cited all sources to acknowledge their contributions.*

*Despite these efforts, the possibility of inadvertent errors remains. I deeply value the insights of my readers and appreciate any feedback that can help identify and rectify such inaccuracies. I encourage you to bring any discrepancies to my attention.*

*Your feedback is not only welcome but crucial, as it will aid in correcting current editions and enhancing the content of future ones. I am committed to maintaining the highest standards of accuracy and reliability in my work and thank you for your support and understanding.*

*Additionally, I firmly uphold the principle of freedom of speech and expression as guaranteed under Article 19(1)(a) of the Constitution of India, and I respect the diverse viewpoints and expressions of all readers.*

ppp

# Other Books Of The Author

1. Empowering Minds: A Journey into Women's Self-Discovery and Power
2. The Dynamics of Motivation: Catalyzing Thought into Action
3. Meditation and Mental Well Being: The Path to Inner Peace and Clarity
4. The Psychology of Child Education: Nurturing Future Generations
5. Ethical Enlightenment: A Modern Guide to Living with Integrity
6. Voices of Empowerment: Stories of Women Rising Against Odds
7. Social Psychology in Everyday Life: Understanding Human Connections
8. The Essence of Motivational Speaking: Inspiring Change in Others
9. Balancing Acts: Women, Work, and the Will to Lead
10. Guiding with Grace: Raising Children with Compassion and Awareness
11. The Power of Positive Aging: Embracing Life After Fifty
12. Building Resilient Communities: Social Work in Action
13. The Ethical Educator: Principles for Teaching and Learning
14. From Insight to Impact: Social Psychology for a Better World
15. The Ethics of Empathy: A Guide to Ethical Living
16. The Science of Empowering the Self: Navigating Life's Challenges with Psychological Wisdom
17. The Mindful Conscious Leader: Meditation Techniques for Modern Management
18. Pioneering Spirit: Women's Pathways to Leadership and Empowerment
19. Feeling to Healing: The Role of Emotional Intelligence in Child Development
20. Transformative Talks and Words of Inspiration: Insights into Motivational Oratory

ﻉﻉﻉ

# Contact


Dr. Minakshi Bansal
Social Activist
Ahmedabad, Gujarat, Bharat
minakshiindiag20@yahoo.com


❧❧❧

|| LOKAHA SAMASTHAHA SUKHINO BHAVANTU ||